American Sublime

. . . .

Other Books by Elizabeth Alexander

POETRY

Antebellum Dream Book

Body of Life

The Venus Hottentot

ESSAYS

The Black Interior

AMERICAN SUBLIME

Poems

Elizabeth Alexander

Graywolf Press

ST. PAUL, MINNESOTA

Publication of this volume is made possible in part by a grant provided by the Minnesota State Arts Board, through an appropriation by the Minnesota State Legislature; a grant from the Wells Fargo Foundation Minnesota; and a grant from the National Endowment for the Arts, which believes that a great nation deserves great art. Significant support has also been provided by the Bush Foundation; Target, with support from the Target Foundation; the McKnight Foundation; and other generous contributions from foundations, corporations, and individuals. To these organizations and individuals we offer our heartfelt thanks.

MINNESOTA
STATE ARTS BOARD

NATIONAL
ENDOWMENT
FOR THE ARTS
A great nation
deserves great art.

Published by Graywolf Press
2402 University Avenue, Suite 203
Saint Paul, Minnesota 55114
All rights reserved.
www.graywolfpress.org

Published in the United States of America

ISBN 978-1-55597-432-9

4 6 8 9 7 5

Library of Congress Control Number: 2005926522

Cover design: Julie Metz
Cover art: *The Annunciation,* Henry Ossawa Tanner
Philadelphia Museum of Art: Purchased with the W. P. Wilstach Fund, 1899

This book is for my mother,
who gave me the word
and keeps our stories alive in her work.

. . . .

Contents

I. American Blue

II. Ars Poetica

III. *Amistad*

IV. American Sublime

I. American Blue
. . . .

Emancipation

Corncob constellation,
oyster shell, drawstring pouch, dry bones.

Gris gris in the rafters.
Hoodoo in the sleeping nook.
Mojo in Linda Brent's crawlspace.

Nineteenth century corncob cosmogram
set on the dirt floor, beneath the slant roof,
left intact the afternoon
that someone came and told those slaves

"We're free."

Little Slave Narrative #1: Master

He would order the women to pull up their clothes
"in Alabama style," as he called it. He would whip them

for not complying. He taught bloodhounds
to chase down negro boys, hence the expression

"hell-hounds on my trail." He was fond of peach brandy,
put ads in the paper: *Search high, search low*

for my runaway Isaac, my runaway Joe,
his right cheek scarred, occasioned by buckshot,

runaway Ben Fox, very black, chunky made,
two hundred dollars live, and if dead,

bring his dead body, so I may look at it.

Ellipsis

White-blossoming trees
in front of the house

in Sparta, Georgia,
where they together lived:

free woman of color
(black, white, Cherokee),

white male slaver,
and their children,

who slept with the mother
in a mouse room connected

to his rooms through secret doors.
He gave his daughters diamonds

which they wore set in rings
on their toes, and hid in their hair.

Distant white relatives
fought for the railroad stock

when he died, and they won.
They also got the house.

You can smell the funk
of the haints in the walls:

mildew, semen, camphor,
oft-handled bills, coin metal,

cornbread breath that whispers
and swallows and breathes.

One day, as in the best
bodice-rippers, the house

burned down to the ground,
burnt down by the distant white cousin

who no doubt heard the ghosts
humming and fussing, rattling,

ratcheting, singing. Burn!
she screamed. So it did.

The fussing quieted. In its place,
wind in the willows, a whiff of

something sweet, something sour,
something always in its place.

Smile

When I see a black man smiling
like that, nodding and smiling
with both hands visible, mouthing

"Yes, Officer," across the street,
I think of my father, who taught us
the words "cooperate," "officer,"

to memorize badge numbers,
who has seen black men shot at
from behind in the warm months north.

And I think of the fine line—
hairline, eyelash, fingernail paring—
the whisper that separates

obsequious from *safe*. Armstrong,
Johnson, Robinson, Mays.
A woman with a yellow head

of cotton candy hair stumbles out
of a bar at after-lunchtime
clutching a black man's arm as if

for her life. And the brother
smiles, and his eyes are flint
as he watches all sides of the street.

Kitchen Portrait, 1971

Wishbone drying on a wall peg,
jar of bacon grease by the stove,
beautiful people the color of that bacon grease:

Mother, color of a calfskin pocketbook,
of a desert, something silvered, "speaks
flawless French." Father, a wishbone,

covered wagon, flag. Two children,
boy-and-a-girl, pancake and butter,
stamp collection and ballet slipper.

Three juices, lined up, three
cereal boxes, and bowls, orange
vitamin pills, blue kitchen stools. School,

job, downtown, carpool,
copper pots, vacuum cleaner,
the narrow countertop where they eat

and things roll off and break sometimes.

Tina Green

Small story, hair story, Afro-American story,
only-black-girl-in-my-class story,
pre-adolescence story, black-teacher story.

"Take your hair out," they beg on the playground,
the cool girls, the straight-and-shiny-hair girls,
the girls who can run.

                    "Take your hair out," they say.
It is Washington hot, we are running, I do,
and it swells, snatches up at the nape, levitates,

woolly universe, knotting, fleece zeppelin, run.
So I do, into school, to the only black teacher
I'll have until college, the only black teacher

I've had to that point, the only black teacher
to teach at that school full of white people
who (tell the truth) I love, the teacher I love,

whose name I love, whose hair I love,
takes me in the teacher's bathroom and wordlessly
fixes my hair, perfectly, wordlessly

fixes my hair into three tight plaits.

When

In the early 1980s, the black men
were divine, spoke French, had read everything,
made filet mignon with green peppercorn sauce,
listened artfully to boyfriend troubles,
operatically declaimed boyfriend troubles,
had been to Bamako and Bahia,
knew how to clear bad humours from a house,
had been to Baldwin's villa in Saint-Paul,
drank espresso with Soyinka and Senghor,
kissed hello on both cheeks, quoted Baraka's
"Black Art": "Fuck poems/and they are useful,"
tore up the disco dance floor, were gold-lit,
photographed well, did not smoke, said "Ciao,"

then all the men's faces were spotted.

Five Elegies

1. Poet's Tale

The older poet, he who would die soon after,
made me swig whiskey from his sacred silver flask
in the dark wings of the famous New York theater
before my maiden performance there, on jazz night,
to honor who else but happy birthday, Doctor King.
The great drummer drummed, great piano player played.
When the young one came out on the bass the older poet
leaned in so close that I could smell the spirits
and whispered, "Don't miss this one. This kid."

                                        He played
and he played, and he was not to be missed, the kid
who played the bass like conjuration. *Don't miss this one,*
and how did he know, the older poet, that I would not miss,
that he was pointing to a man I would love from that night forward.
What did he know when he made me swig for bravery,
pushed me out from behind the black velvet curtains
where I was hiding my face and said "Now"?

2. Lynda Hull

The poet Lynda Hull, who I did not know well,
has died so of course I am remembering
first meeting her in the women's room of an Italian
restaurant in Chicago, where she spoke to me
in the mirror and said, "Us redheads got to stick together,"
both of us dyed and flagrant, red lipstick,
her miniature body fierce and healing.

Poets are only famous to each other.
She wrote in my copy of *Star Ledger* "Hoping
to spend more time with you in this city of divas
and big shoulders," and now she's gone
out like the meteor she was,
a scarlet hole burning and hissing behind,
leaving this bitch of a world for the next.

3. Dream

The father was not my father, rather
a dark-skinned negro TV actor who plays
mid-level lieutenants, is never in charge.
I am me, as are the children, as is mother,
whose face tightens and pales as I diminish.
In my close-up in the hospital corridor
I ask, What is wrong with me? Say, Tell me
how to fight. I have looked in the mirror,
seen my ravages, the face that time and again
will not do what I ask it to, the caul.
The sympathetic negro taps my temple to say,
This kind, he means of cancer, exits weeping.
Time for the terrible aria, the one where I say,
I CAN NOT LEAVE THEM, my children,
and THE ONLY THING I EVER WAS AFRAID OF,
which is almost true.

> The poet Agha Shahid Ali
met that disease and then like a rose
blown open faced his death and died
after asking, in the shape of a poem,
Why must we ever?

4. Ornette Coleman and Thelonious Monk at Dinner

When people smoked, and it hung over the table like magic
or like wisps of the talk and the music between them,

chicken bones, the best Chateaux, Coca-Cola in glass, Monk's eyes
cut left, Ornette laughing at something off-camera,

safari suit and Savile Row bespoke, haberdashery
circa '72 and the black globe is damn near free.

Deep sounds in the cusp and shift, in the sour and the off-notes
you bang and you blow, in the butter, the biscuits, the bird carcass,

jelly, just what you wanted and all you can eat.

. . . .

5. Billy Strayhorn Writes "Lush Life"

Empty ice-cream carton
in a kitchen garbage can.
Up all night with your mother.
He beat her again. Up all night
eating ice cream, you made your mother laugh.

        ly
Life   is lone

Duke's hands on your shoulders,
you play it again. Cancer
eats moth holes through
you and you and you.

        ly
Life   is lone

Speeding upstate in the backseat,
on the Taconic, cocktail
in one hand, book in another
as autumn leaves blur by.
This life, New York, piano,
love, then lonely, this life, love.

Morning, Gordontown

In Jamaican sunlight
roosters crow and tree frogs
peep and yardies shout.

I scoop a divine Bombay mango,
imagine my grandfather's morning
on this soil a century ago.

Etheridge Knight, from prison,
was right: that ancestry
is always an idea

(though kin are real).
But that idea is intimate
(if not precise), distilled

as a drop of the Olbas
menthol oil (a West Indian
secret) my hostess proffers

for a stubborn catarrh
my first night in Jamaica,
on my pillowcase.

Claustrous Euphobia

blue, blue, blue

locked trunk, organized
the old life and me

"sometimes you stay too long
waiting on that exit interview"

: the talk you imagine
will set the record straight

the man and I sat at the kitchen table
for four hours unbroken as I waited

confession   why
fabulous truth imagined

years later I dream him
returning to find me at my childhood home

"I'm sick," he said
"a disease called claustrous euphobia"

which explained everything!
disease, truth- and heart-loving termite

could be six months, six years, six,
looking just as he did on a windy Chicago corner

before and after haircuts,
how he kept his dresser drawers,

ankle brace, Brilliantine, toothpicks,
how he slept, did not snore,

eschewed red meat,
eggs runny, sunny-side up,

other things I have forgotten
on purpose, by mistake

it sometimes leads to blue.

The End

The last thing of you is a doll, velveteen and spangle,
silk douponi trousers, Ali Baba slippers that curl up at the toes,
tinsel moustache, a doll we had made in your image
for our wedding with one of me which you have.
They sat atop our coconut cake. We cut it
into snowy squares and fed each other, while God watched.

All other things are gone now: the letters boxed,
pajama-sized shirts bagged for Goodwill, odd utensils
farmed to graduating students starting first apartments
(citrus zester, apple corer, rusting mandoline),
childhood pictures returned to your mother,
trinkets sorted real from fake and molten
to a single bar of gold, untruths parsed,
most things unsnarled, the rest let go

save the doll, which I find in a closet,
examine closely, then set into a hospitable tree
which I drive past daily for weeks and see it still there,
in the rain, in the wind, fading in the sun,
no one will take it, it will not blow away,

in the rain, in the wind,

it holds tight to its branch,

then one day, it is gone.

Matrimonio

1. Blues

If I am the baby who does not fit
in the overhead compartment, in
the weekender tote, if I am the baby
who will bounce off a lap on the jitney,
who sleeps in a dresser drawer or shoebox,
then I am no rosebud, no foundling, no pearl.
I am outsized, enormous for a baby,
too giant for footie pajamas
(the cradle wood splits, the tree bough breaks),
not baby then but mother, a mama
for whom there is no cupped palm, no bosom,
no cradle, no lap, just the wide world
to be crossed in strides, and the floorboards
to be paced until they wear away to dust.

2. Oscar de la Renta

Oscar de la Renta
adores my avoirdupois,
every ounce, every pouf of me.

His voice never raises,
all sentences prefaced
My darling, My dear.

He's arranged for his best seamstress
to measure and tuck. In a few
weeks' time, the gown will be ready.

He will escort me into Society.
We'll eat a light dinner
on trays, in the library, before.

How he loves
bacon, lettuce,
and tomato sandwiches!

Even in this field of plenty
(my real life, my marriage),
a cold wind blows sometimes

—raised voices, sharp words—
and in dances Oscar de la Renta
to do the Continental

and each time, I give him my hand.

3. The Dancers Dressed in White

It was the dancers dressed in white running
in a line together like spume to the shore
who made me run to where they were, bringing
the baby along in a grocery cart,
distracting him with bananas. There
I made a mistake, soul-kissed the man
who gave me armfuls of dresses, a green dress,
(I never believed I could wear green) kissing
his mouth, making plans to follow him and dance.
Shuck the corn, harvest jig, and I have erred,
but I have not worn white in a century,
not kissed, not danced, not maiden, nor autumn gold
nor spring, nor run full out to the shoreline,
its white edges always receding.

4. Siesta

The sounds of the day turned to dust, particles
fizzing in a sunlight shaft, faraway
lawn mowers, leaf-blowers, motorcar motors,

and the purr of each baby in his sleep,
and Papa's snores, and the tick-tock clock—
even Doña on the bed with Papa,

the kitchen floor swept, food set in the cupboard,
hyacinth nipped and in water releasing
its wild musk throughout the quiet house.

Even Doña has taken her shoes off,
lain down on the bed, and fitted the arch
of her foot in her husband's, and slept.

Krishna Denies Eating Mud

Blue boy, the apple
of his mother's ravening eye.

> *Blue as the noon sky,*
> *Blue as the sea,*
> *Beautiful Krishna*
> *Come to me!*

The boy eats rocks, eats nails,
great fistfuls of mud.

Mother pries the bud-mouth open
and looks inside: a globe,

planets, oceans, telescopes,
Milky Way, books,

beasts, flowers, vegetables,
minutes, time, history,

the universe in Krishna's mouth!
Mother faints, astonished.

Krishna: You will remember none of this.

Mother (awakening): *Angel, blue angel,*
> *Come sit on my lap,*
> *Come sit on my starry skirt.*

Ode

I love all the mom bodies at this beach,
the tummies, the one-piece bathing suits,
the bosoms that slope, the wide nice bottoms,
thigh flesh shirred as gentle wind shirrs a pond.

So many sensible haircuts and ponytails!
These bodies show they have grown babies, then
nourished them, woken to their cries, fretted
at their fevers. Biceps have lifted and toted

the babies now printed on their mothers.
"If you lined up a hundred vaginas,
I could tell you which ones have borne children,"
the midwife says. In the secret place or

in sunlight at the beach, our bodies say
This is who we are, no, This is what
we have done and continue to do.
We labor in love. We do it. We mother.

Stray

On the beach, close to sunset, a dog runs
toward us fast, agitated, perhaps feral,
scrounging for anything he can eat.
We pull the children close and let him pass.

Is there such a thing as a stray child? Simon asks.
Like if a mother had a child from her body
but then decided she wanted to be a different child's mother,
what would happen to that first child?

The dog finds a satisfying scrap and calms.
The boys break free and leap from rock to rock.
I was a stray man before I met your mother,
you say, but they have run on and cannot hear you.

How fast they run on, past the dark pool
your voice makes, our arms which hold them back.
I was a stray man before I met you,
you say. This time you are speaking to me.

Fried Apples

I saw my mother's father
but a few times in my life:

a large man who glittered
and made his own weather,

lived near, rarely visited,
died when I was ten.

The first time I became
a woman I thought I did not

want to know what he taught me
about loving a glittering man.

I became a woman again
and remembered my grandfather

standing at the stove, cooking
a pan of fried apples for us

one Sunday morning in summer,
and I began to take his measure.

The Dream That I Told My Mother-in-Law

In the room almost filled with our bed,
the small bedroom, the king-sized bed high up
and on casters so sometimes we would roll,
in the room in the corner of the corner
apartment on top of a hill so the bed would roll,
we felt as if we might break off and drift,
float, and become our own continent.
When your mother first entered our apartment
she went straight to that room and libated our bed
with water from your homeland. Soon she saw
in my cheeks the fire and poppy stain,
and soon thereafter on that bed came the boy.
Then months, then the morning I cracked first one
then two then three eggs in a white bowl
and all had double yolks, and your mother
(now our mother) read the signs. Signs everywhere,
signs rampant, a season of signs and a vial
of white dirt brought across three continents
to the enormous white bed that rolled
and now held three, and soon held four,
four on the bed, two boys, one man, and me,
our mother reading all signs and blessing our bed,
blessing our bed filled with babies, blessing our bed
through her frailty, blessing us and our bed,
blessing us and our bed.

                        She began to dream
of childhood flowers, her long-gone parents.
I told her my dream in a waiting room:
a photographer photographed women,
said her portraits revealed their truest selves.
She snapped my picture, peeled back the paper,
and there was my son's face, my first son, my self.
Mamma loved that dream so I told it again.

And soon she crossed over to her parents,
sisters, one son (War took that son.
We destroy one another), and women came
by twos and tens wrapped in her same fine white
bearing huge pans of stew, round breads, homemade wines,
and men came in suits with their ravaged faces
and together they cried and cried and cried
and keened and cried and the sound
was a live hive swelling and growing,
all the water in the world, all the salt, all the wails,
and the sound grew too big for the building and finally
lifted what needed to be lifted from the casket and we quieted
and watched it waft up and away like feather, like ash.
Daughter, she said, when her journey began, *You are a mother now,
and you have to take care of the world.*

Black Poets Talk about the Dead

"Like Toni," he said,
"who came plain as day
to my dream last night
in a gangster beret,
tangerine-colored suit,
thigh-high go-go boots,
she tipped that brim and said,
How ya like me now?

"After Etheridge passed
I went to see his woman
with my daughter, who was six
at the time, and had loved him.
We slept in the room where he'd slept
and in the night my child woke up
and said, *I was talking
to Etheridge just now.
Can't you smell his cigarettes?*"

"After she left us, we felt Mom close—
she had passed but not crossed—
and those were good weeks.
Her soup in the freezer,
perfume in her handkerchiefs,
half-empty cups of her tea, grown cold.
But bit by bit she left and then was gone.
They do that so we can mourn.
They do that so we believe it.
It is what it is: wretched work,
that we who the dead leave behind must do."

Notes From

We are Underground. Underground:
a cinder-block barrack, red clay warren,
at times a seaside cottage far away.
Austere and opulent, spartan and lush,
where we struggle to hear ourselves think.
It is not '45, when the A-bomb was dropped
(kimono flowers burned onto skin, shadows
remaindered on walls after bodies disintegrate),
not '55 when Emmett Till was lynched,
nor '63, when the Birmingham church girls
were blown to smithereens (and hear now the sister
who survived, now in her fifties, tell of the dress sash
she was in the midst of tying, of her glass eye
that pops out and rolls across the room),
not '65, when Malcolm, not '68, when King,
when My Lai, not and not and not but now,
which is why we are down in the Underground:

Sun Salutation at dawn, we fill our lungs
with available air and light, exhale
the detritus, breathe in again. How much light
does a bomb flash make, and what can it do?
Can it photostat a body with kimono print?
Today, the Vietnam hero reveals his Bronze Star
was won by ordering civilians shot
as his men escaped the village. The village woman
says she saw her sisters and brothers and mothers
and aunts lined up and shot into a pile. Who
is surprised to hear how war medals are won?
Underground, analysis must overcome surprise.

In Chicago, Girl X who can no longer speak
tells a courtroom in nods and grunts what happened
and who dragged and raped and beat her
out of herself, so she forgot it, until
smoke from a magician's act at school
reminded her of his smell, and the rest.

What reminded the war hero thirty years later
that he ordered a village slaughtered?
His absent leg tells us what we want
war heroes to say. We are Underground
because twelve-year-old boys are sent to prison
for the rest of their lives and eighteen-year-olds
recruited to "guard" them, and dead children

are "collateral damage" to the homegrown bomber
who will sit in the electric chair on television
so a public can watch him blaze out, and find succor.
Too many people have seen too much
and lived to tell, or not tell, or tell
with their silent, patterned bodies,
their glass eyes, gone legs, flower-printed flesh,
ropey scar tissue, nods and grunts, tics and eczemas.
Under, then, under the front porch, in the loam
of the burning and smoking land, the de-
foliated, under that pyre of bones, we scrabble,
and struggle together to hear ourselves think.

The African Picnic

World Cup finals, France v. Brasil.
We gather in Gideon's yard and grill.
The TV sits in the bright sunshine.
We want Brasil but Brasil won't win.
Aden waves a desultory green and yellow flag.
From the East to the West to the West to the East
we scatter and settle and scatter some more.
Through the window, Mamma watches from the cool indoors.

Jonah scarfs meat off of everybody's plate,
kicks a basketball long and hollers, "goal,"
then roars like the mighty lion he is.
Baby is a pasha surrounded by pillows
and a bevy of Horn of Africa girls
who coo like lovers, pronounce his wonders,
oil and massage him, brush his hair.
My African family is having a picnic, here in the USA.

Who is here and who is not?
When will the phone ring from far away?
Who in a few days will say good-bye?
Who will arrive with a package from home?
Who will send presents in other people's luggage
and envelopes of money in other people's pockets?
Other people's children have become our children
here at the African picnic.

In a parking lot, in a taxi-cab,
in a winter coat, in an airport queue,
at the INS, on the telephone,
on the cross-town bus, on a South Side street,
in a brand-new car, in a djellaba,
with a cardboard box, with a Samsonite,
with an airmail post, with a bag of spice,
at the African picnic people come and go.

The mailman sees us say good-bye and waves
with us, good-bye, good-bye, as we throw popcorn,
ululate, ten or twelve suitcases stuffed in the car.
Good-bye, Mamma, good-bye—
The front door shut. The driveway bare.
Good-bye, Mamma, good-bye.
The jet alights into the night,
a huge, metal machine in flight,
Good-bye, Mamma, good-bye.
At the African picnic, people come and go
and say good-bye.

First Word of the Mass for the Dead

As there is such a thing as
the end of a line,

the elders whose passing
occasions the congregation to say,

They don't make them like that anymore,
(Walter Warren Harper, Zememesh Berhe, Gwendolyn Brooks)

you think of the elders still walking
for whom you hold your breath

and write but do not speak those names

so Him-with-the-Square-Toes
(Zora Neale Hurston) perhaps will forget

the street name, house number,
not this one this time.

It only postpones the next berefting.
Where did my grandfather secret

his ring of gold keys?
What is sewn into his mattress?

And no one, no one asked
his mother's name, so there is now

no name for me to write.

Autumn Passage

On suffering, which is real.
On the mouth that never closes,
the air that dries the mouth.

On the miraculous dying body,
its greens and purples.
On the beauty of hair itself.

On the dazzling toddler:
"Like eggplant," he says,
when you say "Vegetable,"

"Chrysanthemum" to "Flower."
On his grandmother's suffering, larger
than vanished skyscrapers,

September zucchini,
other things too big. For her glory
that goes along with it,

glory of grown children's vigil,
communal fealty, glory
of the body that operates

even as it falls apart, the body
that can no longer even make fever
but nonetheless burns

florid and bright and magnificent
as it dims, as it shrinks,
as it turns to something else.

II. Ars Poetica

. . . .

Ars Poetica #10: Crossing Over

Like the low Shaker cradle
sized for a diminished adult
in which they rocked their elderly to death,

or the five evangelical nurses
who sang the Jewish woman to the precipice
then told her to let go, go to Jesus
in a humming circle.

Like the mother of two sons
who sent them away
so they would not see
their mother die,

who refused the Shaker cradle.

Like you, like our mother,
who kept us as close for as long as she could
then sent us away
so she could.

Ars Poetica #1,002: Rally

I dreamed a pronouncement
about poetry and peace.

"People are violent,"
I said through the megaphone

on the quintessentially
frigid Saturday

to the rabble stretching
all the way up First.

"People do violence
unto each other

and unto the earth
and unto its creature.

Poetry," I shouted, "Poetry,"
I screamed, "Poetry

changes none of that
by what it says

or how it says, none.
But a poem is a living thing

made by living creatures
(live voice in a small box)

and as life
it is all that can stand

up to violence."
I put down the megaphone.

The first clap I heard
was my father's,

then another, then more,
wishing for the same thing

in different vestments.
I never thought, why me?

I had spoken a truth
offered up by ancestral dreams

and my father understood
my declaration

as I understood the mighty man
still caught in the vapor

between this world and that
when he said, "The true intellectual

speaks truth to power."
If I understand my father

as artist, I am free,
said my friend, of the acts

of her difficult father.
So often it comes down

to the father, his showbiz,
while the mother's hand

shapes us, beckons us
to ethics, slaps our faces

when we err, soothes
the sting, smoothes the earth

we trample daily, in light
and in dreams. Rally

all your strength, rally
what mother and father

together have made:
us on this planet,

erecting, destroying.

Ars Poetica #17: First Afro-American Esperantist

Gumbo ya-ya, lingua franca,
truffle or frango. Epic,
Affrilachia.

                 Oh language,
my trinket, my dialect bucket,
my bracelet of flesh.

Certificate: Esperantist.
Heirloom trunk, then Beinecke.
X-ray. Communicado. Acid-free.

Ars Poetica #28: African Leave-Taking Disorder

The talk is good. The two friends linger
at the door. Urban crickets sing with them.

There is no *after* the supper and talk.
The talk is good. These two friends linger

at the door, half in, half out, 'til one
decides to walk the other home. And so

they walk, more talk, the new doorstep, the
nightgowned wife who shakes her head and smiles

from the bedroom window as the men talk
in love and the crickets sing along.

The joke would be if the one now home
walked the other one home, where they started,

to keep talking, and so on: "African
Leave-Taking Disorder," which names her children

everywhere trying to come back together and talk.

Ars Poetica #3: Ablutions

The bathroom, its ill-painted windowsills
peeling and chipping, a slow-draining sink,

toiletries lined on the ledge, footstool
for climbing to brush pebble teeth,

the pump-bottle soap, the overflowing
laundry basket of wee socks, large shirts stained

with small prints—
                    After my children have graduated

from evening baths to morning showers
I will still wash their feet in that bathtub

at bedtime, as mine were once washed, as you
washed the nuns' feet in a white enameled basin

as they passed by your home in the Horn of Africa on Maundy Thursdays.

Ars Poetica #85:
Modjadji V the Rain Queen Dies in South Africa at 64

Young people, she complains,
have lost touch with religion,
and no one ever asks me to make rain.

Ars Poetica #23: "Whassup G?"

From the Latin *negrorum,* meaning
"to tote," said Richard Pryor
in an etymological mode.

Look it up in Cab Calloway's
Hepster's Dictionary, that giant book.
Be negro, be 'groid, be vernacular, be.

Hey, yo, Hey bro', Hey blood,
high five, big ups, gimme some skin,
keep it on the QT, the down low, the real side.

What it is? What it look like?
Vernacular: Verna, a house-born slave.
Ask your mama what it means.

Old school lyin' and signifyin'.
That chick has a chemical deficiency:
no assatol.

       And who knows,
on the radio, *what evil lurks*
in the hearts of men? The shadow do,

quoth the brethren, and fall out,
cack-a-lacking and slapping,
high-top fade to black.

Ars Poetica #21: Graduate Study of Literature

Shoebox full of chicken.
Darned sock, repaired picket fence.
A red front yard singing,
geranium pots lined up.

Pennies rolled and ready,
canvas tote bag of second-hand books.
Baltimore Avenue Trolley,
tofu from the corner Koreans.

Mending pile, hand-wash pile,
dry clean pile, Salvation Army pile.
Read so much you need new glasses.
Geraniums in the front yard singing:

"I am hand-made! I am home-grown!
You have not come outside in three days!"
Wash yourself in the following order:
face, pits, puss, behind.

Look inside my workman's lunch pail:
hard-boiled egg, salt in a tinfoil square.
Carrot sticks, nectarine, chicken leg,
chocolate chip cookie or brownie.

Books, books, and talking about them.
Books, books, and talking about them,
and trolleying home to a third floor
walk-up and looking out the window

with bad eyes that can nonetheless
see the red of the geraniums,
the street pageantry that sings
and shuns, summons and sends away.

Ars Poetica #227: Provenance

Coretta
Malcolm

Do your very best
Try, try again

The Bump
The Latin Hustle

Myrlie Evers
Betty Shabazz

Nixon, Agnew
J. Edgar Hoover

Crispus Attucks
Harriet Tubman

The North Star
North

The black cat bone
Room 222

Ron Dellums
Charles Rangell

Shirley Chisolm
Free Angela

Hot breakfast
Prepare

Alberto VO5
Vitapointe

Ebony-JET headquarters
Stocking cap

Twice as good
Wear an extra layer

Valhalla
Harlem

Ars Poetica #92: Marcus Garvey on Elocution

Elocution means to speak out.
That is to say, if you have a tale to tell,
tell it and tell it well.

This I was taught.

To speak properly you must have sound and good teeth.
You must have clear nostrils.
Your lungs must be sound.
Never try to make a speech on a hungry stomach.

Don't chew your words but talk them out plainly.
Always see that your clothing is properly arranged before you get on a platform.
You should not make any mistake in pronouncing your words
because that invites amusement for certain people.

To realize I was trained for this,
expected to speak out, to speak well.
To realize, my family believed
I would have words for others.

An untidy leader is always a failure.
A leader's hair should always be well kept.
His teeth must also be in perfect order.
Your shoes and other garments must also be clean.
If you look ragged, people will not trust you.

My father's shoe-shine box:
black Kiwi, cordovan Kiwi,
the cloths, the lambswool brush.

My grandmother's dressing table:
potions for disciplining
anything scraggle or stray.

For goodness sake, always speak out,

said Marcus Garvey,
said my parents,
said my grandparents,
and meant it.

Ars Poetica #56: "Bullfrogs Was Falling Out of the Sky"

(Bundini Brown)

Not frogs but bullfrogs,
not rain but fat rain,
not Congo but Zaire
and Mobutu Sese Seko,

Mobutu Sese Seko,
his solid gold toilet seat,
leopard-skin fez,
international airstrip.

Not stealing but plundering,
Not Congo, Zaire. Not Drew
but Bundini, not Baptist
but Jew.

Not Cassius,
Muhammad, not Jesus
but Allah, the Koran,
the Bible, the Bible is black.

Do like it says on the mayonnaise jar:
keep cool but do not freeze.
Do like it says on the mayonnaise jar,
keep cool but do not freeze.

Not Afro but Afri-
ca, booty but plunder,
rain that astonishes,
rain like bullfrogs.

Mobutu, Mobutu,
both booty and plunder.
Oh Africa, Africa,
God in the rain.

Ars Poetica #16: Lot

During the Middle Passage
the captives drew lots for everything—

rations, labor, sleeping space—

I drew a laminated card
that read "Countee Cullen."

Here I am.

Ars Poetica #13: The Idea of Ancestry

Ralph Ellison's house is underground
next door to my house. Somehow we
buried it during the renovation.
The stream of which he wrote, the lullaby
sung softly by its banks is the one
my children sing, in tongues.

Ralph Ellison had an outside child—
shh—it is whispered, but when
will someone tell me the full story?
We buried his house under cast-off
sheetrock, beams, and broken appliances.

Walk in my flowering peony bed
and you'll find it, a TV antenna
made from a bent wire hanger:
what's left of Ralph Ellison's house.
It picks up mysterious whispers.

Ars Poetica #2: Christening

We pour radiant water
on a rosebush

off the walking path,
water from the baby's bath

the third day after
christening. He'd wailed

in the tiled font, then
came to us serene,

tonsured, agleam
with holy oil, damp

with sacred water,
in his new white clothes.

We waited three days.
We bathed the luminous child.

We saved that precious water.
We sanctified the roses.

Ars Poetica #336: Rose-Colored Glasses

Mom said, Sometimes I dream we reclaim the apartment
which is even more beautiful than it was then, and perfect

where you swung on a trapeze in the dining room archway
played checkers with a dolly big enough to be your sister
plink-plinked on the piano your little dog's nails scritch-scratching
the hardwood floors when he heard you walking from the elevator
where there was no divorce there was no desperation where

one day you would cut off your two long braids and your mother would save them.

Ars Poetica #66: How To

(found poem)

American Judo
How to Fight
America's Swimming Primer

Police Jujitsu
Police Wrestling
Scientific Boxing

How to Dance
Tip Top Tapping
Swing Steps

Famous Cowboy Songs
Famous Old Time Songs
Gipsy Luck Dream Book

Joe Miller's Joke Book
How to Make Funny Gags
Laughter for the Millions

Spanish Self-Taught
French Self-Taught
Polish Self-Taught

Common Sense in Chess
Champion Checkers
Mechanical Air-Conditioning

25 Lessons in Hypnotism
Telling Fortunes by Cards
How to Become an American Citizen

Mermaid's Guide to True Love

. . . .

Ars Poetica #37: Patriarchy

(at the Peabody Museum)

Who's bigger,
Daddy, or the bear?

Ars Poetica #100: I Believe

Poetry, I tell my students,
is idiosyncratic. Poetry

is where we are ourselves
(though Sterling Brown said

"Every 'I' is a dramatic 'I'"),
digging in the clam flats

for the shell that snaps,
emptying the proverbial pocketbook.

Poetry is what you find
in the dirt in the corner,

overhear on the bus, God
in the details, the only way

to get from here to there.
Poetry (and now my voice is rising)

is not all love, love, love,
and I'm sorry the dog died.

Poetry (here I hear myself loudest)
is the human voice,

and are we not of interest to each other?

Ars Poetica #88: Sublime

In a pickle, we talk our way out
of our corners. We can the rough stuff.
Overture, theme and variation,
call and response, "I" equals "we."

Girl could *talk*. Sweet or savory?
Nutmeg or cinnamon? Jalapeno
or scotch bonnet? Maraschino
cherry or angostura bitters?

Sing, your mouth an O
which bubbles, tra la la,
or reaches low
to where *Nobody knows.*

What a baby knows:
the word as light,
the word as vowel,
the word as element,

the need to sing.

III. *Amistad*

. . . .

Amistad

After the tunnel of no return
After the roiling Atlantic, the black Atlantic, black and mucilaginous
After skin to skin in the hold and the picked handcuff locks
After the mutiny
After the fight to the death on the ship
After picked handcuff locks and the jump overboard
After the sight of no land and the zigzag course
After the Babel which settles like silt into silence
and silence and silence, and the whack
of lashes and waves on the side of the boat
After the half cup of rice, the half cup of sea-water
the dry swallow and silence
After the sight of no land
After two daughters sold to pay off a father's debt
After Cinque himself a settled debt

After, white gulf between stanzas

the space at the end

the last quatrain

The Blue Whale

swam alongside the vessel for hours.
I saw her breach. The spray when she sounded
soaked me (the lookout) on deck. I was joyous.
There her oily, rainbowed, lingering wake,
ambergris print on the water's sheer skin,
she skimmed and we skimmed and we sped
straight on toward home, on the glorious wind.

Then something told her, Turn (whales travel
in pods and will beach themselves rather than split)—
toward her pod?—and the way she turned was not
our way. I begged and prayed and begged for her
companionship, the guide-light of her print,
North Star (I did imagine) of her spout.
But she had elsewhere to go. I watched
the blue whale's silver spout. It disappeared.

Absence

In the absence of women on board,
when the ship reached the point where no landmass
was visible in any direction
and the funk had begun to accrue—
human funk, spirit funk, soul funk—who
commenced the moaning? Who first hummed that deep
sound from empty bowels, roiling stomachs,
from back of the frantically thumping heart?
In the absence of women, of mothers,
who found the note that would soon be called "blue,"
the first blue note from one bowel, one throat,
joined by dark others in gnarled harmony.
Before the head-rag, the cast-iron skillet,
new blue awaited on the other shore,
invisible, as yet unhummed. Who knew
what note to hit or how? In the middle
of the ocean, in the absence of women,
there is no deeper deep, no bluer blue.

boy haiku

the motherless child
rests his hand on a dead man's
forehead 'til it cools.

Poro Society

Without leopard skin, leather,
antelope horns, wart-hog tusks,
crocodile jaws, raffia muffs,

without the sacred bush,
the primordial grove,
our ancient initiations,

we must find a way
to teach the young man
on board with us.

We contend
with the forces of evil
in the universe.

Aggressive magic
addresses the need for control
in an imperfect world.

Approach

With shore in sight, the wind dies and we slow.
Up from the water bobs a sleek black head
with enormous dark eyes that question us:

who and what are you? Why? Then another
and another and another of those
faces, 'til our boat is all surrounded.

The dark creatures are seen to be
seals, New England gray seals, we later learn.
They stare. We stare. Not all are blackest black:

some piebald, some the dull gray of the guns
our captors used to steal and corral us,
some the brown-black of our brothers, mothers,

and two milky blue-eyed albino pups.
Albino: the congenital absence
of normal pigmentation. Something gone

amiss. Anomaly, aberration.

Connecticut

They squint from shore
at scarlet-shirted blackamoors.

The battered boat sails in.
White sky, black sea, black skin,

a low black schooner,
armed black men on deck

in shawls, pantaloons,
a Cuban planter's hat—

parched, starved,
dressed in what they found

in the dry goods barrels,
the Africans squint

at trees not their trees,
at shore not their shore.

Other Cargo

Saddles and bridles,
bolts of ribbon,
calico, muslin, silk,
beans, bread, books,
gloves, raisins, cologne,
olives, mirrors, vermicelli,
parasols, rice, black bombazine.

Education

In 1839, to enter University,
the Yale men already knew Cicero,

Dalzel's *Graeca Minora*, then learned more Latin prosody,
Stiles on astronomy, Dana's mineralogy.

Each year they named a Class Bully
who would butt heads with sailors in town.

"The first foreign heathen ever seen,"
Obookiah, arrived from Hawaii in '09.

The most powerful telescope in America
was a recent gift to the school

and through it, they were first to see
the blazing return of Halley's comet.

Ebeneezer Peter Mason
and Hamilton Lanphere Smith

spent all their free time at the instrument
observing the stars, their systems,

their movement and science and magic,
pondering the logic of mysteries that twinkle.

Some forty years before, Banneker's
eclipse-predicting charts and almanacs

had gone to Thomas Jefferson
to prove "that nature has given our brethren

talents equal to other colors of men."
Benjamin Banneker, born free,

whose people came from Guinea,
who taught himself at twenty-two (the same age

as the graduates) to carve entirely from wood
a watch which kept exquisite time,

accurate to the blade-sharp second.

The Yale Men

One by one the Yale men come
to teach their tongue to these
caged Africans so they might tell

in court what happened on the ship
and then, like Phillis Wheatley,
find the Yale men's God

and take Him for their own.

Teacher

(Josiah Willard Gibbs)

I learn to count in Mende one to ten,
then hasten to the New York docks to see
if one of these black seamen is their kind.

I run to one and then another, count.
Most look at me as though I am quite mad.
I've learned to count in Mende one to ten!

I shout, exhausted as the long day ends
and still no hope to know the captive's tale.
Is any of these black seamen their kind?

I'd asked an old Congo sailor to come
to the jail, but his tongue was the wrong one,
I learned. To count in Mende one to ten

begin *eta, fili, kian-wa, naeni.*
I spy a robust fellow loading crates.
Is this the black seaman who is their kind?

He stares at me as though I am in need,
but tilts his head and opens up his ear
and counts to me in Mende one to ten,
this one at last, this black seaman, their kind.

Translator

(James Covey)

I was stolen from Mendeland as a child
then rescued by the British ship *Buzzard*
and brought to Freetown, Sierra Leone.

I love ships and the sea, joined this crew
of my own accord, set sail as a teen,
now re-supplying in New York Harbor.

When the white professor first came to me
babbling sounds, I thought he needed help
until *weta,* my mother's *six,* hooked my ear

and I knew what he was saying, and I knew
what he wanted in an instant, for we had heard
wild tales of black pirates off New London,

the captives, the low black schooner like
so many ships, an infinity of ships fatted
with Africans, men, women, children

as I was. Now it is my turn to rescue.
I have not spoken Mende in some years,
yet every night I dream it, or silence.

To New Haven, to the jail. To my people.
Who am I now? This them, not them. We burst
with joy to speak and settle to the tale:

We killed the cook, who said he would cook us.
They rubbed gunpowder and vinegar in our wounds.
We were taken away in broad daylight.

And in a loud voice loud as a thousand waves
I sing my father's song. It shakes the jail.
I sing from my entire black body.

Physiognomy

Monday, September 16, 1839

*Another of the captured Africans named Bulwa (or Woolwah) died
on Saturday night. This is the third who has died in this city, and
the thirteenth since their leaving Havana. One more remains sick in
this city, the others having been removed to Hartford on Saturday, to
await their trial on Tuesday the 17th. Several are still affected with
the white flux, the disease which has proved fatal to so many of them.*

The Daily Herald, New Haven

Kimbo, 5 feet 6 inches, with mustaches and long beard,
in middle life, calls himself Manding. Very intelligent,

he counts thus: 1. *eta,* 2. *fili,* 3. *kian-wa,* 4. *naeni,*
5. *loelu,* 6. *weta,* 7. *wafura,* 8. *wayapa,*
9. *ta-u,* 10. *pu.*

Shuma, 5 feet 6 inches, spoke
over the corpse of Tha
after Reverend Mister Bacon's prayer.

Konoma, 5 feet 4 inches, with incisor teeth
pressed outward and filed, with large lips
and projecting mouth, tattooed on the forehead,

calls himself Congo (Congo
of Ashmun's map of Liberia,
or Kanga, or Vater).

They are represented by travelers as handsome.
They are supposed to be more ancient of the soil than Timaris.
Their language, according to Port Chad, is distinct from any other.

Biah, 5 feet 4-1/2 inches with remarkably pleasant countenance,
with hands whitened by scars from gunpowder,
calls himself Duminah (Timari),

counts also in Timari.
He counts in Bullom thus.
He counts in Manding like Kwong.

With face broad in the middle
With sly and mirthful countenance (rather old)
With full Negro features
With hair shorn in rows from behind
With permanent flexion of two fingers on right hand
A mere boy, calls himself Manding
With depression of skull from a forehead wound
Tattooed on breast
With narrow and high head
With large head and high cheekbones
Marked on face by the smallpox
Stout and fleshy

Teme, 4 feet 3 inches, a young girl,
calls herself Congo but when further interrogated
says her parents were Congo, she a Manding.

Observe that in this examination
no one when asked for his name
gave any other than an African name.

No one when asked
to count counted in any
language other than African.

There was no appearance in any of them,
so far as I could judge,
of having been from Africa more than two or three months.

Constitutional

Mary Barber's children beg their mother
to take them into town each day to see
the Africans on the New Haven Green
let out of their cells for movement and air.

A New York shilling apiece to the jailer
who tucks away coins in a full suede purse.
The children push through skirts, past waistcoats,
to see the Africans turn somersets.

In the open air, in the bright sunlight,
the Africans chatter, and sound to
the children like blackbirds or cawing gulls.
The Africans spring. The Africans do not smile.

Mende Vocabulary

they
my father
our father
your father
my mother
our mother
my book
his house
one ship
two men
all men
good man
bad man
white man
black man

I eat
he eats
we eat
they sleep
I see God
did I say it right?
we sleep
I make
he makes
they have eaten

this book is mine
that book is his
this book is ours
I am your friend
here
now
that
there
then

The Girls

Margru, Teme, Kere,
the three little girls onboard.
In Connecticut
they stay with Pendleton
the jailer and his wife.
Some say they are slaves
in that house. The lawyer
comes to remove them,
but they cling to their hosts,
run screaming through the snow
instead of go. Cinque comes
and speaks in their language
with much agitation.
Do you fear Pendleton? *No.*
Do you fear the lawyer? *No.*
Do you fear Cinque? *No.*
Who or what do you fear?
The men, they say, *the men.*
The girls will become Christians.
They will move to Farmington
with the Mende mission
and return to Sierra Leone.
One will return to America
to attend college at Oberlin.
They will be called Sarah,
Maria, and Charlotte.

Kere's Song

My brother would gather the salt crust.
My grandmother would boil it gray to white.

My mother boated in the near salt river,
grabbed fat fish from the water with bare hands.

Women paint their faces with white clay and dance
to bring girls into our society, our

secrets, our womanhood, our community.
The clay-whitened faces of my mothers

are what I see in my dreams, and hear
drum-songs that drown girls' cries after

they have been cut to be made women.
If someone does evil, hags ride them

all night and pummel them to exhaustion.
Hags slip off their skins and leave them

in the corner during such rambles.
At my grandmother's grave, cooked chicken, red rice,

and water to sustain her on her journey.
I was learning the secrets of Sande

when they brought me here, before my dance,
before my drum, before my Sande song.

Judge Judson

These negroes are *bozals*
(those recently from Africa)
not *ladinos*

(those long on the island)
and were imported
in violation of the law.

The question remains:
What disposition shall be made
of these negroes?

Bloody may be their hands
yet they shall
embrace their kindred.

Cinqueze and Grabeau
shall not sigh for Africa
in vain

and once remanded
they shall no longer
be here.

In Cursive

Westville, February 9, 1841

Miss Chamberlain and others,

I will write you a few lines
because I love you very much
and I want you to pray to the great God to make us free
and give us new souls and pray for African people.

He sent his beloved son into the world
to save sinners who were lost. He sent
the Bible into the world to save us
from going down to Hell, to make us turn from sin.

I heard Mr. Booth say you give five dollars
to Mr. Townsend for African people. I thank you
and hope the great God will help you and bless you
and hear you and take you up to Heaven when you die.

I want you to pray to the great God make us free.
We want to go home and see our friends in African Country.
I want the great God love me very much and forgive all my sins.
All Mendi people thank you for your kindness.

Hope to meet you in Heaven. Your friend, Kale

God

There is one God in Farmington, Connecticut,
another in Mendeland.

None listen.
None laugh, but none have listened.

We will sail home carrying Bibles
and wearing calico.

The journey this time
is seven weeks.

If we find our mothers,
children, fathers, brothers,

sisters, aunties, uncles,
cousins, friends,

if we find them,
we will read to them

(we read this book)
the God stories in our Bibles.

That is the price for the ticket home
to Mendeland

for us the decimated three years hence.

Waiting for Cinque to Speak

Having tried,

having tried, having failed,

having raised rice
that shimmered green, green,
having planted and threshed.

Having been a man, having sired children,
having raised my rice, having amassed a bit of debt,
having done nothing remarkable.

Years later it would be said
the Africans were snatched into slavery, then,
that we were sold by our own into slavery, then,
that those of our own who sold us
never imagined chattel slavery,
the other side of the Atlantic.

Having amassed debt, I was taken to settle that debt.
(Not enough rice in the shimmering green.)
Better me than my daughter or son. (I was strong.)
And on the ship I met my day
as a man must meet his day.
Out of the Babel of Wolof and Kissee
we were made of the same flour and water, it happened.
On the ship, I met my day.

The *Amistad* Trail

The *Amistad* Trail bus
leaves from the commuter parking lot,
Exit 37 off Highway 84.
There is interest in this tale.

See where the girls lived while waiting
for the boat to sail home, see Cinque's room,
the Farmington church where they learned
to pray to Jesus, Foone's grave.

Good things: eventual justice, John Quincy Adams,
black fighting back, white helping black.
Bad things: the fact of it, price of the ticket,
the footnote, the twist, and the rest—

Done took my blues
Done took my blues and

—the good and the bad of it.
Preach it: learn. Teach it: weep.

Done took my blues.
Done took my blues and gone.
The verse will not resolve.
The blues that do not end.

Cinque Redux

I will be called bad motherfucker.
I will be venerated.
I will be misremembered.
I will be Seng-Pieh, Cinqueze, Joseph,
and end up CINQUE.

I will be remembered
as upstart, rebel, rabble-rouser, leader.
My name will be taken by black men
who wish to be thought RIGHTEOUS.
My portrait will be called "The Black Prince."
Violent acts will be committed in my name.
My face will appear on Sierra Leonean currency.

I will not proudly sail the ship home
but will go home, where I will not sell slaves,
then will choose to sail off
to a new place: Jamaica, West Indies.
In America, they called us *"Amistads."*
The cook we killed, Celestino, was mulatto.
Many things are true at once.

Yes I drew my hand across my throat
in the courtroom, at that cur Ruiz
to hex his thieving, killing self.
Yes I scuffled here and there instead of immolate.
Yes I flaunted my gleam and spring.
No I did not smile.
No I never forgot the secret teachings
of my fathers. No I never forgot

who died on board, who died on land,
who did what to whom, who will die
in the future, which I see
unfurling like the strangest dream.

The Last Quatrain

and where now

and what now

the black white space

IV. American Sublime

· · · ·

American Sublime

(At the same time, American paintings wherein
the biodynamic landscape explodes in flames,

ice, violent sunshine that seems to burn the canvas,
apocalyptic nature that roils and terrifies.

The Beautiful: small scale, gentle luminosity.
Sublime: territorial, vast, craggy, un-

domesticated, borderless, immense, unknown,
awful, monumental, transcendent, transcending.

Go West and West young man, to blinding snowstorms. Leave
shark-infested waters, shipwrecks without slaves.

Miraculous black holes of color large enough
to blot out the sun, obliterate the unending moans,

to exalt, to take the place of lamentation.)

Tanner's *Annunciation*

Gabriel disembodied,
pure column of light.

Humble Mary, receiving the word
that the baby she carries is God's.

Not good news, not news, even,
but rather the rightly enormous word,

Annunciation. She knew
they were chosen. She knew

he would suffer, as the chosen child
always suffers. Perhaps she knew

the dearest wish, mercy,
would be ever-inchoate,

like Gabriel: light that carries
possibility, illuminates,

but that can promise nothing but itself.

Notes

"Amistad"

On July 2, 1839, a rebellion occurred aboard the Spanish slave schooner *Amistad* near the coast of Cuba. The *Amistad* was sailing from Havana to Puerto Principe, Cuba, when the ship's passengers, three girls, one boy, and thirty-nine men recently abducted from Sierra Leone, revolted. The captives, led by Joseph Cinque, killed the ship's captain and cook, but spared the navigator so that he would bring the ship back to Sierra Leone. Instead, the navigator sailed northward, where the United States Navy seized the *Amistad* off Long Island and towed it to New London, Connecticut. The captives were held in a jail in New Haven, Connecticut. There was great interest in their presence, including from Yale Professor Josiah Willard Gibbs, who brought his students to try to teach the captives English so that they might tell their story in court.

The Spanish demanded the return of the *Amistad* captives to Cuba. In 1840, a trial took place in a federal court in Hartford, Connecticut. New England abolitionist Lewis Tappan and others tried to organize sympathy for the captives, but the United States government sided with proslavery opinions. President Martin Van Buren ordered a Navy ship sent to Connecticut to return the Africans to Cuba. Nonetheless, the judge ruled that the captives were not merchandise, but were instead victims of kidnapping and had the right to escape their captors; he said they should be made free. The United States appealed the case before the Supreme Court the next year; congressmen and former president John Quincy Adams argued in favor of the Africans. The Supreme Court upheld the lower court. Private and missionary society donations helped the thirty-five surviving Africans secure passage back to Sierra Leone, where they arrived in January 1842. Five missionaries and teachers hoping to found a Christian mission joined the Africans on this return.

Spain insisted that the United States pay indemnification for the ship. The United States Congress continued to debate the case until the beginning of the Civil War in 1861.

Acknowledgments

These poems have appeared in the following publications, sometimes in different versions:

American Poetry Review: "Ars Poetica #10: Crossing Over"
The Antioch Review: "Emancipation"
The New Yorker: "Autumn Passage," "When," "Smile"
Rattapallax: "Kitchen Portrait, 1971"
Shenandoah: "Lynda Hull"
Souls: "Notes From"
South Atlantic Quarterly: "Amistad"
TriQuarterly: "Ornette Coleman and Thelonious Monk at Dinner"
Water-Stone: "Ode," "The African Picnic"

Grateful acknowledgment is made to the editors of these publications. The author would also like to thank the John Simon Guggenheim Foundation for a grant during which this book was completed.

ELIZABETH ALEXANDER was born in New York City and raised in Washington, D.C. She is the author of four collections of poetry, *The Venus Hottentot*, *Body of Life*, *Antebellum Dream Book*, and *American Sublime*, which was a finalist for the 2005 Pulitzer Prize in Poetry. She is also the author of two collections of essays, *The Black Interior* and *Power and Possibility: Essays, Interviews, Reviews*, and a collection of poems for young adults, *Miss Crandall's School for Young Ladies and Little Misses of Color* (co-authored with Marilyn Nelson). She recently edited *The Essential Gwendolyn Brooks*. She has read her work across the United States and in Europe, the Caribbean, and South America, and her poetry, short stories, and critical prose have been published in numerous periodicals and anthologies. On January 20, 2009, Alexander delivered a poem at the inauguration of President Barack Obama. She is the recipient of the Alphonse Fletcher, Sr. Fellowship for work that "contributes to improving race relations in American society and furthers the broad social goals of the U.S. Supreme Court's Brown v. Board of Education decision of 1954," and the 2007 Jackson Prize for Poetry, awarded by Poets and Writers. Alexander is a professor of African American Studies and American Studies at Yale University, and also teaches in the Cave Canem Poetry Workshop. She lives with her family in New Haven, Connecticut.

American Sublime has been set in Adobe Caslon Pro, an open type version of a typeface originally designed by William Caslon sometime between 1720 and 1766. The Adobe version was drawn by Carol Twombly in 1989.

Book design by Wendy Holdman.
Composition by BookMobile Design and Publishing Services.
Manufactured by Thomson-Shore on acid-free paper.